What You
DON'T KNOW
About

ANIMALS

What You DON'T KNOW About ANIMALS

by Ryder Windham

AN
APPLE
PAPERBACK

SCHOLASTIC INC.

New York   Toronto   London   Auckland   Sydney
Mexico City   New Delhi   Hong Kong   Buenos Aires

For Dorothy and Violet

Special thanks to my editors, David Levithan and Erin Soderberg, and to Karla Moran for her research assistance on raptors.

ISBN 0-439-22533-7

12 11 10 9 8 7 6 5 4   2 3 4 5 6 7/0

Printed in the U.S.A.   40
First Scholastic printing, January 2002

CONTENTS

INTRODUCTION

How many animals have you seen in the wild, in the zoo, and on television? Probably more than you can remember! Scientists have identified more than 1.5 million different animal species, and there are millions more that remain unidentified or undiscovered.

This book features just a few dozen animals, and you'll probably recognize most of them. But do you know which animal is the fastest on two legs, and why gorillas don't drink water? How about whether penguins have knees, or if pandas have thumbs? You'll find the answers to these questions and many more in this book.

AMERICAN ALLIGATOR

SCIENTIFIC NAME: *Alligator mississippiensis* (alligator of Mississippi)

RANGE: southeastern United States from Texas to Florida and north through eastern South Carolina

HABITAT: freshwater rivers, lakes, and swamps

NUMBER OF EGGS: 25 to 60 (up to 45 may hatch)

HATCHLING WEIGHT: 2 ounces

ADULT WEIGHT: 350 to 500 pounds (females are smaller)

LENGTH: 8 to 12 feet

DIET: fish, turtles, snails, snakes, birds, mammals, other alligators, and carrion

LIFE SPAN: 30 to 35 years in the wild; up to 50 years in captivity

PREDATORS: alligator eggs and hatchlings are prey to hawks, herons, and sometimes other alligators. Adult alligators are only preyed upon by humans.

STATUS: once endangered, but not currently endangered

Alligators are members of the order Crocodylia, which also includes crocodiles and gavials. Scientists regard crocodilians as "living fossils" because they have survived on Earth for more than 225 million years. That's longer than the dinosaurs, which became extinct about 65 million years ago! There are 23 species of crocodilians but only two species of alligators: the American alligator and the endangered Chinese alligator.

🐾 The American alligator gets its name from sixteenth-century Spanish explorers, who called it "*el largato*," which means lizard. Non-Spanish explorers and colonists interpreted the name as "alargato," and finally *alligator*.

🐾 A male alligator is called a *bull*. A female alligator is a *sow*. A group of alligators is called a *congregation*.

🐾 A baby alligator is called a *hatchling*. A group of baby alligators is called a *pod*.

🐾 In their wetland habitat, alligators are the predators that come at the top of the food chain. In other words, all their neighbors are lunch!

🐾 A female alligator builds her own nest from leaves, sticks, and mud on or near the water. Her eggs are about the size of chicken eggs.

🐾 An egg's incubation temperature determines the sex of the alligator. Cooler nests (82°–86°F) produce females, warmer nests (90°–93°F) produce males, and temperatures in between will produce a clutch with both sexes. Eggs in the nest's center — the warmest spot — tend to be male.

🐾 Other creatures rely on the female alligator's fierce reputation to defend her nest against predators. Although red-bellied turtles are prey to alligators, they sometimes risk death to lay their eggs in the alligator's nest, hoping she will guard the turtle eggs, too.

🐾 After her eggs hatch, the alligator will protect and care for her young for up to two years. By the standards of the animal kingdom, she's a very caring mother!

🐾 At any given time, alligators have approximately 80 teeth. When the teeth wear down, they are replaced by new ones. An alligator can go through 2,000 to 3,000 teeth in a lifetime! After about 50 years, they run out of teeth and may die of starvation.

☙ Alligators do not chew their food but use their teeth to seize, tear, and crush food before swallowing. Gulp!

☙ An alligator can remain underwater for more than an hour. While submerged, it can open its mouth to capture prey but does not swallow until it surfaces. If it did, it would swallow water along with its prey and choke!

☙ Alligators do not need to eat continuously. During extremely cold weather, they can hibernate for three to five months.

☙ Alligators do not have vocal cords, but males can bellow to attract females, then roar to warn other males to maintain their distance.

☙ In Florida, the heaviest alligator on record was a 1,043-pound male found in Orange Lake.

WHAT'S THE DIFFERENCE BETWEEN ALLIGATORS AND CROCODILES?

Alligators and crocodiles differ in many ways, but you can actually see the difference in their head shape: Alligators have broad, blunt, V-shaped snouts, and crocodiles have U-shaped snouts. When an alligator's mouth is shut, its lower teeth slide up into its upper jaw, so you can't see its lower teeth. When a crocodile's mouth is shut, the large fourth tooth in the lower jaw is visible, extending up alongside its snout.

If you see a crocodilian in salt water, it's likely to be a crocodile, as they have a high tolerance for salt. Although alligators can survive in salt water for brief periods of time, they prefer freshwater because their glands do not secrete salt very well. Many people think that crocodiles are much more aggressive than alligators. Maybe crocodiles should lay off the salt. . . .

Speaking of aggressive behavior, here's something to keep in mind if a crocodilian challenges you to a wrestling match. Crocodilians have strong muscles to close their jaws, but the muscles used to open their mouths are weak. When an alligator's or crocodile's jaws are already closed, it doesn't require much strength for an adult human to hold the reptile's mouth shut. But when you release the jaws, your arms and the rest of your body had better be far, far away from your opponent. On second thought . . . *don't accept wrestling challenges from crocodilians!*

🐾 The longest alligator on record was 19 feet 2 inches. It was killed in Louisiana in 1890 by the naturalist Edward Avery McIlhenny and was probably well over 50 years old since it was almost entirely toothless.

🐾 In 1967 the American alligator was considered an endangered species, and alligator hunting was prohibited. In 1997 alligators were reclassified as threatened but no longer endangered.

🐾 Alligators are not known to attack humans except in self-defense.

🐾 In 1987 the alligator became the official state reptile of Florida.

NILE CROCODILE

SCIENTIFIC NAME: *Crocodilus niloticus* (crocodile of the Nile)

RANGE: tropical and southern Africa and Madagascar

HABITAT: rivers, freshwater marshes, estuaries, and mangrove swamps

NUMBER OF EGGS: 25 to 60 (about 40 will hatch)

HATCHLING WEIGHT: 3 ounces

ADULT WEIGHT: 500 to 1,650 pounds (females are smaller)

LENGTH: 16 to 20 feet

DIET: up to 70 percent of the adult diet is fish; also hippos, porcupines, pangolins, migrating wildebeests, and zebras

LIFE SPAN: 45 years in the wild; up to 80 years in captivity

PREDATORS: eggs and hatchlings are prey to other creatures, such as marabou storks, Nile monitor lizards, and other crocodiles. Adult crocodiles are preyed upon only by humans.

STATUS: not endangered, but very vulnerable to human intrusion

❧ The Nile crocodile is the largest African reptile.

❧ A female crocodile prepares her nest on sandy shores and dry riverbanks and covers her eggs with sand. She digs up the eggs when she hears them hatching.

❧ As with alligator eggs, the incubation temperature of crocodile eggs determines whether the hatchling will be female or male.

❧ After her eggs have hatched, the female crocodile scoops up her hatchlings — about 15 at a time — in her mouth and carries them to the water.

❧ Despite the mother crocodile's careful protection, her eggs and hatchlings are prey to other creatures, such as marabou storks, Nile monitor lizards, and other crocodiles. Only about 2 percent of all Nile crocodile hatchlings reach adulthood.

❧ Adult Nile crocodiles are prey only to human poachers. Otherwise, they are at the top of their food chain.

🐾 Nile crocodiles survive on about 50 full meals a year. They do not hibernate.

🐾 Nile crocodiles have 66 teeth. They also have a special bony throat flap that allows them to eat underwater without swallowing water.

🐾 Do birds make good dentists? Nile crocodiles appear to enjoy having their teeth cleaned by several species of birds, including the Egyptian plover or "crocodile bird." While the crocodiles rest with their mouths open, the birds pick at the food stuck between the crocodiles' teeth. When the birds are done, they fly away!

🐾 Of all animals, crocodiles have the most acidic digestive system. Their stomachs can dissolve bones and horns. No leftovers for dinner!

🐾 Nile crocodiles can swim in bursts of speed up to 29 miles per hour.

SCIENTIFIC NAME: *Pan troglodytes* (a troglodyte is a prehistoric cave dweller)

RANGE: western and central Africa

HABITAT: rain forests and grasslands with trees

YOUNG PER BIRTH: 1

BIRTH WEIGHT: 4 to 5 pounds

ADULT WEIGHT: 60 to 150 pounds (females are smaller)

HEIGHT: 3½ to 5 feet

DIET: omnivorous (fruits, leaves, insects, and sometimes meat)

LIFE SPAN: 30 to 40 years in the wild; more than 50 years in captivity

PREDATORS: humans and leopards

STATUS: endangered

🐾 Chimpanzees are very social animals and live in communities that may average 40 to 60 chimpanzees. Friendly physical contact is important to chimpanzees; such "social grooming" is believed to help them maintain friendships and calm nervous individuals.

🐾 A young chimpanzee will remain with its mother for six to ten years.

🐾 Chimpanzees spend a lot of time on the ground but are considered *arboreal* (tree dwellers). They sleep in nests that they build in high trees, and they make new nests every night.

🐾 Chimpanzees use tools for specific tasks. They use stones to crack open nuts, and twigs to draw ants and termites out of their nests.

🐾 When threatened by leopards or humans, chimps defend themselves by throwing large sticks or using the sticks like clubs.

🐾 How strong are chimpanzees? About five to eight times stronger than humans!

Before human astronauts ventured into space, scientists sent animals to find out whether humans could survive the trip. The first animal launched into Earth's orbit was a dog (you can read about Laika on page 115).

On January 31, 1961, an American Mercury-Redstone 2 rocket blasted off from Cape Canaveral, carrying a 37-pound male chimpanzee. The "astrochimp" was named Ham, in recognition of the *Holloman Aerospace Medical Center*, and he was almost four years old. In preparation for his mission, Ham had received extensive training so his behavior and reflexes could be tested during the flight. When he performed a test correctly, he received a banana pellet; when he failed a test, he received an electric shock.

Within 17 minutes of the launch, the rocket had reached a top speed of 5,857 miles per hour and an altitude of 157 miles; it traveled a total of 422 miles before splashing down into the Atlantic. During the flight, Ham experienced several minutes of weightlessness and became the first chimpanzee in space. How did he do on his tests? He performed about 50 tasks and received only two electric shocks. When Ham's capsule was opened, he was rewarded with an apple and half an orange.

 You might not be a monkey's uncle, but you could be considered an ape's cousin! Genetic research has revealed that chimpanzee DNA and human DNA are 98.4 percent identical, and gorilla DNA and human DNA are 97.7 percent identical. This means that our genetic composition is very similar and that we are slightly more related to chimpanzees than we are to gorillas.

☙ A female chimpanzee named Washoe was the first nonhuman animal to acquire a human language: American Sign Language (ASL). Since 1967 she has been cared for by psychologist Roger Fouts. Washoe's vocabulary includes 240 "reliable" signs (meaning that she has demonstrated them with consistent accuracy), and she has taught her adopted son Loulis to sign as well!

☙ According to the National Wildlife Federation, there were nearly 2 million chimpanzees at the beginning of the twentieth century. In the year 2000 the number of chimpanzees had decreased to approximately 180,000.

MOUNTAIN GORILLA

SCIENTIFIC NAME: *Gorilla gorilla beringei* (named after the German Army officer Captain Oscar von Beringe, who shot two mountain gorillas while he was climbing Mount Sabinyo in 1902)

RANGE: the Bwindi and Virunga mountains of Central Africa

HABITAT: dense forests

YOUNG PER BIRTH: 1

BIRTH WEIGHT: 3 to 4 pounds

ADULT WEIGHT: 300 to 425 pounds

HEIGHT: up to 5½ feet tall

DIET: herbivorous (bamboo, wild celery, fruit, and other vegetation)

LIFE SPAN: 53 years in captivity

PREDATORS: leopards and humans

STATUS: critically endangered

All gorillas come from Africa, and all are endangered. There are three subspecies of gorillas: the Western lowland gorilla, the Eastern lowland gorilla, and the mountain gorilla. The mountain gorilla has adapted to live at higher altitudes, but its characteristics, including longer body hair and larger nostrils, are only slightly different from the lowland gorilla.

- A male gorilla is called a *bull*, and a female is a *sow*. A group of gorillas is a *band*.

- Gorillas live in bands of three to 30 members, which are led by a dominant adult male *silverback*, named for the silvery hairs on his back.

- Like chimpanzees, gorillas spend much of their time grooming one another. Although most movies portray gorillas as fierce creatures, they are really quite shy.

- Gorillas only attack humans when they are provoked. They are very protective of their young and will defend them with their lives.

- Gorillas do not drink water but get all the water they need from eating large amounts of moist vegetation.

- Since gorillas don't drink water, perhaps it's not surprising that they don't know how to swim.

- Smile! Gorillas and humans have the same number of teeth: 32.

- An adult male gorilla consumes about 50 to 60 pounds of food a day. That's like eating 250 quarter-pounders.

- Gorillas wander within a home range of 10 to 15 square miles. Every night, they get ready for "bed" by building a fresh nest of branches or grasses on the ground.

- Mountain gorillas are even more endangered than panda bears. In 1990 it was estimated that there were only 620 mountain gorillas. By 2000 the National Wildlife Federation estimated the population had been reduced to 320.

WHAT'S THE DIFFERENCE BETWEEN APES AND MONKEYS?

Apes are members of the mammal group called *primates*, which also includes monkeys and humans. Together, we primates share a lot of characteristics, such as the basic design of our bodies: two forward-facing eyes, two arms and two legs, opposable thumbs that allow us to grasp objects, fingernails instead of claws, and the ability to stand erect, among others. Unlike other primates, humans don't have opposable toes, which are handy for climbing trees.

Generally, a monkey can be any primate except a human, but people usually say "monkey" when they're talking about long-tailed primates like marmosets and spider monkeys. Apes include the chimpanzee, gorilla, gibbon, and orangutan. In simple terms, monkeys have tails, and apes don't have tails.

A group of monkeys is called a *troop*. A group of apes is called a *shrewdness*.

🐾 Since 1972 psychologist Francine "Penny" Patterson has been teaching a lowland gorilla named Koko a modified form of American Sign Language. Patterson says Koko has a "vocabulary" of more than one thousand gestures and understands more than two thousand words of spoken English.

ORANGUTAN

SCIENTIFIC NAME: *Pongo pygmaeus* (pygmy man-ape)

RANGE: the islands of Sumatra and Borneo

HABITAT: lowland jungles

YOUNG PER BIRTH: 1

BIRTH WEIGHT: 3 to 3½ pounds

ADULT WEIGHT: 80 to 200 pounds (males are heavier)

HEIGHT: 3½ to 4½ feet (males are taller)

DIET: frugivorous (fruit eater — figs, mangoes, and leaves)

LIFE SPAN: 35 years in the wild; 50 years in captivity

PREDATORS: tigers and humans

STATUS: critically endangered

- In Malay, *orang* means person and *utan* means forest.

- Although orangutans can walk upright, their short legs do not support their body weight very well. However, they have extremely powerful arms, which they use for climbing and *brachiating* (swinging from branch to branch).

- More arboreal than chimpanzees, orangutans rarely descend to the forest floor. They are the largest of tree-dwelling mammals. If tigers were walking around in your neighborhood, you'd probably feel safer up in a tree, too!

- Orangutans build their nests, which are made of branches and grasses, in trees, sometimes as high as 70 feet above the ground. They make a new nest every night.

- Unlike other primates, adult orangutans are not very social, prefering to live alone instead of in groups.

- Like chimpanzees, orangutans use sticks and grasses as tools. They use these tools to reach for food or swat snakes.

19

❧ Orangutans sometimes wear large leaves on their heads. Imagine how they'd behave in a hat shop!

❧ Between 1997 and 1998 forest fires destroyed much of the habitat of the already-endangered orangutans, and thousands of them died. In 2000 the National Wildlife Federation estimated the orangutan population to be only 15,000 to 20,000 in number.

GRIZZLY BEAR

SCIENTIFIC NAME: *Ursus arctos horribilis* (horrible or ferocious bear)

RANGE: western Canada and the northwestern United States

HABITAT: tundra, alpine meadows, river valleys, and coastlines

BIRTH WEIGHT: 12½ to 14 ounces

ADULT WEIGHT: 300 to 1,000 pounds (females are smaller)

HEIGHT: 3 to 3½ feet at the shoulder. When standing on their hind legs, males can be 8 to 10 feet and females about 7 feet.

LENGTH: up to 7 feet from nose to rump

DIET: omnivorous (deer, moose, fish, and vegetation)

LIFE SPAN: 25 to 30 years in the wild; more than 40 years in captivity

PREDATORS: habitat loss and humans

STATUS: threatened

Estimates suggest there may have been more than 100,000 grizzly bears throughout the western half of North America in the early nineteenth century, but their numbers were diminished by hunting and habitat loss.

In 2000 the National Wildlife Federation estimated there were about 31,700 grizzly bears in Alaska, approximately 25,000 in Canada, and fewer than 1,000 in Alaska, Wyoming, Idaho, and Montana.

* Grizzly bears are large brown bears but are often considered a separate species. The largest brown bear is the Kodiak, which can weigh up to 1,500 pounds.

* Male grizzlies are called *boars*, and females are *sows*. Young bears are *cubs*. A group of bears is a *sloth*.

* The grizzly bear has 42 teeth: 12 incisors, 4 canines, 16 premolars, and 10 molars. Bears are the only large predators that regularly eat both plants and meat.

* Grizzlies eat 25 to 35 pounds of food a day. In late summer and early fall, when they are

preparing for hibernation, they gain as much as 40 pounds a week.

* Most female bears give birth to two or three baby cubs at a time. The cubs are born blind and without hair or teeth. During their birth, their mother is usually in hibernation, sound asleep.

* Grizzly cubs nurse from their sleeping mother. In spring, when the mother's hibernation ends, the cubs weigh an average of 50 to 60 pounds.

* During hibernation, a male grizzly bear loses between 15 percent and 30 percent of his weight, and a female grizzly with newborn cubs loses up to 40 percent of her weight.

* Although grizzly bears do attack humans, it's usually because the humans are trespassing on their territory.

BEARS

Bears live all over the world, except Africa, Antarctica, and Australia. There are eight species in the bear family: American black bears, brown bears (large brown bears are known as grizzly bears), polar bears, giant panda bears, Asiatic black bears, sloth bears, spectacled bears, and sun bears.

The smallest bear is the sun bear, which weighs about 100 pounds. Polar bears are the largest bear and also the largest living carnivores! All bears are *plantigrade* (flat-footed), with five toes on each foot, and they walk on the entire foot, just like humans. This might not sound so unusual until you consider that many other animals walk on their toes.

KEEP AWAY FROM WILD BEARS!

What are the chances of a person being killed by a bear? According to a survey of deaths that occurred in Yellowstone National Park between 1839 and 1994, five people were killed by bears and five people were struck by lightning. Does this mean a person is about as likely to be killed by a bear as struck by lightning? Yes, at least at Yellowstone National Park.

Most bears want nothing to do with humans, but they don't like strangers blundering around their territory. If you're hiking through bear country, there are a few steps you can take to help prevent an encounter with a wild bear.

1. As you walk, look around. Don't just stare at the ground in front of you.
2. Keep your food in plastic containers, and don't leave any food lying around.
3. Tie bells to your shoes so bears can hear you approach. You don't ever want to surprise a bear!

WHAT IS HIBERNATION?

In winter, when trees have lost their leaves and various prey have migrated, it is difficult for most creatures to find food. Some animals conserve energy and prevent starvation by placing themselves in a dormant state called *hibernation*, a deep, deep sleep that can last for months.

In the bear family, only brown bears, American black bears, Asiatic black bears, and pregnant female polar bears hibernate (male polar bears remain active all year-round). The other bear species live in warmer habitat zones and can find food throughout the year.

Bears prepare for hibernation by consuming food — much more than usual — that will greatly increase their body fat. During hibernation, their bodies continue to be nourished by their fat resources. They also prepare their den, often in a cave, burrowed hole, or hollow tree cavity. When bears hibernate, their heartbeats drop from 40 to 70 beats per minute to only 8 to 12 beats per minute. Bears do not eat, drink, or excrete during hibernation, and their body temperatures drop only slightly, which allows them to wake up quickly if necessary.

POLAR BEAR

SCIENTIFIC NAME: *Ursus maritimus* (sea bear)

RANGE: Canada, Alaska, Russia, Greenland, and Norway

HABITAT: Arctic coast and ice floes

YOUNG PER BIRTH: usually 2

BIRTH WEIGHT: 21 to 25 ounces, about the size of a chipmunk!

ADULT WEIGHT: 660 to 1,300 pounds (females are smaller)

HEIGHT: up to 4 feet at the shoulder

LENGTH: 6½ to 10 feet

DIET: carnivorous (seals, young walruses, and stranded whales)

LIFE SPAN: 15 to 18 years, but some more than 25 years

PREDATORS: other polar bears and humans

STATUS: no special status

❧ Six of ten polar bear cubs die within their first year. Some starve because their mothers don't feed them, or they die in accidents. Others are killed by human hunters or adult male polar bears. Their lives depend entirely on how well their mother protects them and trains them to survive.

❧ The record weight for an adult male polar bear is more than 2,200 pounds.

❧ A polar bear's stomach can hold more than 150 pounds of food.

❧ Of all bear species, polar bears have the keenest sense of smell. They can smell a seal that is a half mile away and in a breathing hole three feet beneath the snow!

❧ A polar bear's foot pad has tiny suction cups that prevent the bear from slipping on ice.

❧ Polar bears can maintain an average swimming speed of 6 miles per hour for more than 60 miles without requiring rest. For short distances, polar bears can swim up to 25 miles per hour.

❖ Although polar bear fur appears white, it is actually transparent and without color. Each hair shaft has a hollow core that reflects visible light, much like snow and ice.

❖ In 1979 three polar bears at the San Diego Zoo appeared to turn green after the hollow hair shafts of their fur became the temporary home to colonies of algae. After the algae were killed with a salt solution, the bears' fur returned to normal.

❖ The skin under a polar bear's fur is black. Scientists believe the dark skin allows the bear to retain heat.

PANDA BEAR

SCIENTIFIC NAME: *Ailuropoda melanoleuca* (*Ailuropoda* means cat-footed and *melanoleuca* means black and white)

RANGE: mountainous areas of southwestern China

HABITAT: dense bamboo forests

YOUNG PER BIRTH: 1 or 2 cubs, but usually only 1 survives

BIRTH WEIGHT: about 3.7 ounces, lighter than an apple!

ADULT WEIGHT: 175 to 275 pounds (females are smaller)

HEIGHT: up to 32 inches at the shoulder, and up to 67 inches when standing

LENGTH: 5 to 6 feet from nose to rump

DIET: although panda bears are biologically carnivorous, they have adapted to an almost entirely vegetarian diet that is 95 to 99 percent bamboo

LIFE SPAN: 10 to 15 years in the wild, and more than 20 years in captivity

PREDATORS: humans and leopards

STATUS: extremely endangered, primarily because of habitat loss

The existence of pandas was not known to westerners until 1869, when Chinese hunters presented a dead panda to the French missionary Armand David. David sent the pelt to Paris for examination, and the "discovery" of this new species caused a sensation. The great panda's remote, mountainous habitat made expeditions to see it both difficult and expensive.

For more than a century, many scientists believed panda bears were not really bears at all but were more closely related to raccoons, like the red panda. It was only in the 1980s that DNA testing confirmed that pandas are indeed members of the bear family.

🐾 Also known as great pandas, panda bears were once kept as pets by Chinese emperors.

🐾 Bamboo isn't very nutritious, so pandas eat a lot of it in order to get the nutrients they need. Each day, panda bears feed for 10 to 16 hours, consuming 20 to 40 pounds of bamboo leaves and stems or up to 84 pounds of bamboo shoots.

🐾 Do pandas have thumbs? Not exactly. Pandas have five toes on their front paws, but they also have a fleshy pad that extends from their wrist bones. Just as we use our thumbs to grasp objects, pandas use their padded wrist bone for grasping bamboo.

☙ Panda bears can stand, but cannot walk, on their hind legs. They are playful and like to perform somersaults.

☙ Wild panda bears do not have dens. After they're done eating, they just lie down and go to sleep beside a convenient tree.

☙ By the late 1930s the Chinese government realized the panda required protection from foreign hunters. Since 1939 China has prohibited the capture of giant pandas. Currently, all pandas outside China are either gifts or on loan from the Chinese government.

☙ The oldest captive giant panda on record was 37-year-old DuDu, who died in 1999 at China's Wuhan Zoo.

☙ Since 1987 China has imposed the death penalty for anyone convicted of killing or smuggling a giant panda or its skin. Despite this severe law, criminals continue to kill pandas because their skins fetch a high price on the black market.

SU-LIN, FIRST LIVE PANDA IN AMERICA

In 1934 the American explorer William Harvest Harkness, Jr., went to China to capture a live panda for the Brooklyn Zoo, but he died in Shanghai in 1936. Harkness's widow, clothing designer Ruth Harkness, left New York and went to China to resume the hunt.

On November 9, 1936, one of Ruth Harkness's native guides found an infant panda that was approximately ten days old and weighed about 3 pounds. Believing the panda to be female, Harkness named it Su-Lin, which means "little bit of something very cute" in Chinese.

Ruth Harkness brought Su-Lin back to America, making Su-Lin the first live panda to be taken from China. The Brooklyn Zoo was reluctant to accept the panda, apparently because the animal's health was in question.

Su-Lin died on April 1, 1938, at Chicago's Brookfield Zoo. The cause of Su-Lin's death was attributed to an infection that had set in after the panda swallowed an oak twig that had to be surgically removed from her throat. Su-Lin's autopsy revealed that "she" was actually a male panda. At the time of his death, Su-Lin was approximately 17 months old.

NORTH AMERICAN BISON

SCIENTIFIC NAME: *Bison bison* (variation of German *wisesnt*, an ox-like animal)

RANGE: western North America

HABITAT: prairie, grassland, and open woodland

YOUNG PER BIRTH: 1, rarely 2

BIRTH WEIGHT: 40 to 50 pounds

ADULT WEIGHT: 700 to 2,200 pounds (females are smaller)

HEIGHT: 5 to 6 feet

BODY LENGTH: 7 to 13 feet

TAIL LENGTH: 3 feet

DIET: herbivorous (grasses and leaves)

LIFE SPAN: 30 years and older

STATUS: classified as a low-risk, conservation-dependent species by the International Union for Conservation of Nature and Natural Resources (IUCN)

The French called North American bison *boeufs*, meaning oxen or beefs; Anglo-Americans translated this term as *buffalo*. Although bison are commonly referred to as buffalo, they are not related to the oxlike buffalo of Africa.

Historically, bison were revered by Native Americans, who hunted them sparingly and utilized almost every part of the animal's body. The meat of bison provided food, and their skins were transformed into clothing and shelter. Sinew was used as sewing thread and bowstring, bones were shaped into tools, untanned hide (rawhide) was stretched to secure war clubs to handles, and dried dung was used to fuel fires.

It is estimated that more than 40 million bison roamed North America before European colonization. Unfortunately, nineteenth-century colonists and explorers began killing millions of bison for their skins alone, and millions more were killed for sheer sport. In fact, railroad companies encouraged travelers to shoot bison from train windows.

In May 1894 Congress enacted a law to make buffalo hunting illegal in Yellowstone National Park. By 1895 naturalist writer Ernest Thompson Seton could verify the existence of only 800 bison in America and Canada. President Theodore Roosevelt and Congress were persuaded to set aside lands for the preservation of the American bison. Between 1907 and 1909 three reserves were established to save bison from extinction. Today at least 250,000 bison live in North America. They are no longer considered endangered.

🐾 A male bison is a *bull*. A female bison is a *cow*. A young bison is a *calf*. A group of bison is called a *herd* or *troop*.

🐾 A newborn calf will stand within 30 minutes of birth and walk within a few hours. A bison reaches maturity at three years.

🐾 Bison are the largest land mammals in North America. They are the only mammals that do not contract cancer.

🐾 Despite their size, bison are capable of jumping over 6-foot fences. They are also good swimmers.

🐾 Bison can run at speeds near 30 miles per hour. They can outrun and outmaneuver most horses.

🐾 Bison horns have a bony interior, which is covered by an exterior of specialized hair follicles, similar to human fingernails. Unlike antlers, bison horns are never shed and continue to grow throughout the bison's life.

 A bison's tail is considered a warning flag. When the tail dangles and switches naturally, the bison is relaxed. If it juts out and droops at the end, the bison is becoming agitated. When it sticks straight up, the bison is preparing to charge.

 Protected by their thick skin, bison can endure the harshest weather. They do not need or seek shelter.

 Bison drink water once a day. In winter, they eat snow.

THE BUFFALO NICKEL

In 1911 U.S. Secretary of the Treasury Franklin MacVeagh commissioned sculptor James Earle Fraser to design a new nickel. The coin's obverse (front) featured a profile of a Native American man. The coin's reverse (back) bore an image of a bison, drawn from a photograph of Black Diamond, a bison bull that had been born and raised in New York's Central Park Zoo. Although most coins are identified by their obverse image, the new five-cent piece — released in 1913 — became known as the "buffalo nickel."

The buffalo nickel lasted until 1938, when it was replaced by the Thomas Jefferson nickel.

DOMESTIC CHICKEN

SCIENTIFIC NAME: *Gallus domesticus* (domestic cock)

HABITAT: family and factory farms

NUMBER OF EGGS: about 12

HATCHLING WEIGHT: 1½ ounces

ADULT WEIGHT: 4 to 7 pounds

HEIGHT: 12 to 15 inches

DIET: grains and insects

LIFE SPAN: up to 15 years, unless the chicken is bound for a supermarket

PREDATORS: humans

STATUS: not threatened by extinction

There are more than 60 breeds of domestic chickens, and all have a common ancestor: the red jungle fowl, which still exists in the wilds of Southeast Asia. The word *domesticated* means that the animal is trained or tamed to live within a household or farm environment. Historic records indicate that chickens were domesticated in China and Egypt more than 3,000 years ago.

Chickens are bred for their eggs and meat. It is estimated that humans eat more than 73 billion pounds of chicken meat every year.

- A male chicken is a *cock* or *rooster*. A female chicken is a *hen*. A group of hens is called a *flock* or *brood*.

- A baby chicken is a *chick*. A group of chicks is called a *peep* or *clutch*.

- A young female chicken is a *pullet*. A young male chicken is a *cockerel*.

- Chickens that are used for egg or meat production are called *poultry*.

☙ How old is a hen before she begins to lay eggs? Eighteen to 22 weeks.

☙ Hens can produce eggs without a mate. However, only eggs that are produced by mating will yield chicks.

☙ It takes a hen 24 to 26 hours to lay an egg. The egg incubates for 21 days before the chick hatches.

☙ Chickens grow very fast. It only takes about seven weeks for a 1½-ounce chick to become a 4½-pound chicken.

☙ After hens are 10 to 18 months old, they produce fewer eggs. These hens are slaughtered and sold as stewing hens.

☙ Chickens have distinctive fleshy growths on their body. Their head is topped by a red *comb*, and two red *wattles* dangle below the beak. Combs and wattles are red because they are rich in blood.

✿ Chickens have four-toed feet, which gives them a good grip on the ground. Some domestic breeds can fly short distances, but most are bred to be so heavy that they can't fly at all.

✿ The average American eats about 245 eggs and 23 chickens every year.

SCIENTIFIC NAME: *Phoenicopterus ruber ruber* (red red flamingo)

RANGE: Bahamas, Caribbean, Galápagos, northern South America, and the Yucatán

HABITAT: hypersaline lagoons, mudflats, and salt lakes

NUMBER OF EGGS: 1

HATCHLING WEIGHT: 3 ounces

ADULT WEIGHT: 6½ to 8 pounds (females are slightly smaller)

HEIGHT: 43 to 51 inches

WINGSPAN: 55 to 65 inches

DIET: herbivorous (red algae, aquatic invertebrates, and small fishes)

LIFE SPAN: 20 years in the wild; more than 40 years in captivity

PREDATORS: humans

STATUS: not endangered; protected as nongame birds

There are five species of flamingos: the greater flamingo (which includes the subspecies American flamingo and Caribbean flamingo), Chilean flamingo, Andean flamingo, James's flamingo, and lesser flamingo. Of all the species, the greater flamingo has the widest distribution, and the American flamingo is the largest in size.

All flamingos have a long, flexible neck and a distinctive curved bill that is used to suck in water and filter out minute crustaceans that make up much of their diet. Their long legs allow them to wade through marshes.

🐾 Male and female flamingos take turns incubating their egg. The yolk of a flamingo egg is red.

🐾 A newly hatched flamingo chick is gray or white.

🐾 In the wild, pink flamingos are pink because of what they eat. Their diet of algae and shellfish is rich in *carotene*, the pigment that gives the pink color to salmon, shrimp, and lobster.

🐾 In zoos, most flamingos eat food that is mixed with Flamen oil, a blend of carrot oil and other vegetable oils. Without that dietary color additive, "pink flamingos" in the zoo would be white!

🐾 Flamingos are among the few creatures that have adapted to live in volcanic lake environments, where the only freshwater comes from hot geysers. Incredibly, they are capable of drinking water that is almost boiling!

🐾 The flamingo has the longest tongue of all birds.

🐾 Flamingos stand on one leg when they rest. By holding the other leg close to their bodies, they keep one foot warm and also conserve their body heat.

🐾 When you look at flamingos' legs, do you think the position of their knees makes their legs look "backward"? Think again! A flamingo's knees are located very close to the bottom of its body, and are not visible externally. The joints that appear to be the flamingo's knees are actually its ankles. So what do they walk on? Their toes!

SCIENTIFIC NAME: *Struthio camelus* (camel-like ostrich)

RANGE: East Africa

HABITAT: open country and dry savannah

NUMBER OF EGGS: no easy number here! A female ostrich lays 2 to 12 eggs over a three-week period, but a group of ostriches share a communal nest, with an average of 10 to 40 eggs per nest. However, the dominant female will decide which eggs will be incubated. Only about 10 percent of the eggs will hatch.

HATCHLING WEIGHT: 2½ pounds

ADULT WEIGHT: 250 to 345 pounds (females are smaller)

HEIGHT: 8 to 9 feet

DIET: herbivorous (leaves, flowers, shoots, and seeds)

LIFE SPAN: 40 years and more in the wild; more than 80 years in captivity

PREDATORS: Egyptian vultures, hyenas, and jackals

STATUS: not currently endangered

- Ostrich eggs are the largest of any living bird. The average ostrich egg is about 5 to 6 inches in diameter and weighs approximately 3 pounds, which is equal to about 24 chicken eggs. An ostrich egg's shell is about six one-hundredths of an inch thick, but the egg is so strong that it will not break under the weight of an adult human.

- The largest ostrich egg on record measured 7 inches by 4½ inches.

- The yolk of an ostrich egg is the largest single cell of any existing organism.

- Ostrich chicks are about 1 foot tall. When they're four weeks old, they can already run 35 miles per hour!

- Despite their speed, young ostriches are prey to many animals. It is estimated that 15 percent do not survive their first year.

- How fast does a young ostrich grow? About a foot a month! At that rate, they reach their full height in just a few months.

- An ostrich's eye is larger than its brain. Each eye weighs just over 2 ounces, which is more than four times the weight of a human eye!

- Ostriches have excellent vision, which — combined with their height and flexible necks — makes them something like living periscopes. They can see predators coming from more than 2 miles away.

- When ostriches are scared, do they hide their heads in the sand? Only in cartoons! But to evade detection from predators, ostriches will lie motionless on the ground.

- *Beep beep!* If a roadrunner raced an ostrich, who would win? It's no contest. A roadrunner runs about 15 miles per hour, and an adult ostrich can run up to 44 miles per hour. In fact, the ostrich is the fastest animal on two legs!

- An ostrich is the only two-toed bird. Its larger inner toe is tipped with a long, sharp claw. When attacked, an ostrich can launch a kick so deadly that it is capable of disemboweling a lion.

ADÉLIE PENGUIN

SCIENTIFIC NAME: *Pygoscelis adeliae* (Adélie penguin)

RANGE: Antarctica

HABITAT: ice floes

NUMBER OF EGGS: 2

HATCHLING WEIGHT: about 5.3 ounces

ADULT WEIGHT: 11 to 12 pounds (females are slightly smaller)

HEIGHT: 28 inches

WING LENGTH: 8 to 9 inches

DIET: krill, squid, and mollusks

LIFE SPAN: 15 to 20 years

PREDATORS: leopard seals, killer whales, and skuas

STATUS: not endangered, and protected by the Antarctic Conservation Act

There are 17 species of penguins, and their natural habitat is south of the equator. The Adélie penguin's conservational status is considered stable, but most other penguin species are either vulnerable, threatened, or endangered.

Although some penguins live on tropical islands, the Adélie — like the larger emperor penguin — lives in Antarctica. These flightless birds are all adapted for swimming and cold-water diving.

 The word *penguin* may be derived from the Latin word *pinguis*, which means fat. Then again, it may come from the Welsh *pen gwen*, which means white head.

 A group of penguins is a *colony*.

 Adélie penguins were named by the French explorer Jules-Sébastien-César Dumont d'Urville, who first sighted them in January 1840. He named them after his wife.

 Adélie penguins build their nests out of small stones and pebbles. They use their beaks to carry the rocks, one at time. Because rocks are difficult to find in Antarctica, penguins often fight and steal the rocks from one another.

🐾 Female and male Adélie penguins share the responsibility of incubating (warming by sitting on) their eggs and raising their young.

🐾 You might have heard that penguins waddle because they don't have knees. Penguins *do* have knees, but they walk on their haunches, with their knees tucked up in front of their chests. When penguins jump or swim, you can see their legs, knees and all.

🐾 Most birds walk on their toes, but penguins walk on the soles of their feet, just like humans!

🐾 To survive freezing air and water temperatures, penguins have an insulating layer of fat and waterproof feathers.

🐾 Using their wings like flippers, Adélie penguins can propel their torpedo-shaped bodies through the water at about 6 miles per hour. This speed gives them enough momentum to leap up to 4 feet out of the water so they can jump onto ice floes and rocky shorelines.

🐾 Adélie penguins can dive to depths of 295 feet and stay underwater for up to three minutes. They have solid, heavy bones, which help them stay submerged.

🐾 If you ever see a penguin anywhere near a polar bear, you're probably in a zoo or watching a cartoon. Penguins come from the Southern Hemisphere, and polar bears are from the Northern Hemisphere, so you won't ever see them together in the wild.

SCIENTIFIC NAME: *Haliaeetus leucocephalus* (sea eagle with a white head)

RANGE: throughout North America, but most abundant in Canada and Alaska

HABITAT: lakes, large rivers, and coastlines

NUMBER OF EGGS: 1 to 3, but usually only 1 eaglet is raised

HATCHLING WEIGHT: 4 ounces

ADULT WEIGHT: 8 to 14 pounds (females are larger)

HEIGHT: 3 feet from head to tail

WINGSPAN: up to 90 inches

DIET: carnivorous (fish, waterfowl, and carrion)

LIFE SPAN: up to 30 years in the wild; more than 50 years in captivity

PREDATORS: humans

STATUS: threatened

Before European colonists arrived in North America, bald eagles thrived on both the Atlantic and Pacific coasts and nested in what would eventually become 45 of the lower 48 states. On June 20, 1782, Congress approved the bald eagle as the national emblem of the United States of America. Benjamin Franklin — who had previously proposed a rattlesnake for the emblem — was opposed to the eagle and would have preferred the turkey, which he thought was "a much more respectable Bird." Because of the bald eagle's practice of taking fish from fishing hawks, Franklin believed eagles possessed "bad moral character."

Many Americans agreed. Farmers were angry when bald eagles killed their livestock, and they appealed to the U.S. government. By the end of the nineteenth century, federal agencies paid bounties of up to two dollars for every dead bald eagle.

In 1940 Congress passed the Bald Eagle Protection Act, which made it illegal to harm, kill, or possess an eagle, living or dead. But the new law did not prevent the distribution of toxic pesticides such as dichlorodiphenyltrichloroethane (DDT), used to kill insects. The bald eagles preyed on animals that had eaten the poisoned insects, and the toxins caused female bald eagles to lay thin-shelled eggs that broke before they hatched. Also, the Bald Eagle Protection Act only applied to the United States. The territory of Alaska did not become a state until 1959, and between 1917 and 1953, hunters killed more than 100,000 bald eagles there.

In 1967 the U.S. Secretary of the Interior listed the bald eagle as endangered. In 1973 lawmakers created the Endangered Species Act, and the bald eagle became an internationally protected animal. Fortunately, conservation efforts worked. In 1995 the U.S. Fish and Wildlife Service reclassified bald eagles from endangered to threatened. Today it is estimated that there are 50,000 bald eagles in the United States, 80 percent of which are in Alaska. The U.S. Fish and Wildlife Service has proposed that bald eagles be reclassified as fully recovered, but this decision is still pending. Even if bald eagles are declared fully recovered, they will still be protected by federal law.

🐾 There are four groups of eagles: booted eagles, fish eagles, giant forest eagles, and snake eagles. Bald eagles are fish eagles.

🐾 The head of a bald eagle is covered with dark feathers when it is young and white feathers when it matters. The eagle's name is derived from the Old English word *balde*, which means white.

 Bald eagles are *diurnal*, that is, they are active between sunrise and sunset.

 A bald eagle's vision is about four times more powerful than perfect human vision. Flying several hundred feet over water, they can easily sight individual fish.

 A bald eagle's skeleton weighs about 8 ounces, and the bones are hollow. Much of the bald eagle's weight is from its feathers — approximately 7,000 in all! Because the feathers overlap and provide warmth, bald eagles can survive cold weather, but they migrate if waters freeze and food becomes scarce.

 Bald eagles can fly at 20 to 40 miles per hour and dive for prey at speeds up to 100 miles per hour. Flying bald eagles use their tail feathers like a brake when they want to land.

RAPTORS

Birds that eat other animals are called *birds of prey*. Since robins eat worms, you could call a robin a bird of prey, but finding and eating a worm doesn't necessarily make a bird into a great hunter. If you've ever swallowed a worm, you know what I mean.

The most skilled birds of prey are called *raptors*, which include accipiters, buteos, eagles, falcons, ospreys, owls, and vultures. These predatory birds are characterized by superb vision; excellent hearing; a sharp, hooked beak; and clawed feet called *talons*, which are used for grabbing prey. In Latin, the word *raptor* means one who seizes.

There are 59 species of eagles in the world and more than 200 species of owls. North America is home to two species of eagles — the bald eagle and golden eagle — and 18 species of owls, including the great horned owl.

- Not only do bald eagles fish, they swim, too, moving their wings in a fashion that resembles the butterfly stroke.

- A bald eagle's talons and beak are made of keratin and grow continuously, just like human hair and fingernails.

- Bald eagles spend a good deal of time adding branches to their nests. Nests range from 5 to 9 feet in diameter, and some weigh more than 2 tons. If the nest is in a high tree or on a cliff, it is called an *aerie*. Some bald eagles build their nests on the ground.

Young eagles are called *eaglets*. It's not unusual for an eaglet — especially a female — to kill a younger sibling while their parents just sit in the nest and watch. Yikes! I'd rather have alligators for parents.

Ten to 14 weeks after hatching, an eagle prepares to fly from the nest. Forty percent of all bald eagles do not survive their first flight.

Although it is generally illegal to possess any part of an eagle, permits may be granted to use eagles for scientific purposes or for Native American cultural purposes.

During America's Civil War, a bald eagle named Old Abe (after President Abraham Lincoln) became the mascot for the Eighth Regiment of the Wisconsin Volunteer Infantry. When the "Eagle Regiment" engaged in battle, one soldier was assigned to protect Old Abe from Confederate gunfire.

Following the war, Old Abe lived as a celebrity in the state capitol in Madison until 1881, when a small fire broke out near his room. Old Abe was not burned, but he became ill from the smoke and died. He was more than 21 years old. His body was stuffed and put on display in the capitol, but it did not survive a more devastating fire that destroyed the capitol in 1904.

SCIENTIFIC NAME: *Bubo virginianus* (owl discovered in Virginia)

RANGE: throughout North America

HABITAT: forests, prairies, parks, and cities

NUMBER OF EGGS: usually 2 or 3

HATCHLING WEIGHT: 0.13 ounces

ADULT WEIGHT: 2½ to 3½ pounds (females are larger)

HEIGHT: 18 to 22 inches

WINGSPAN: 4 to 6 feet

DIET: birds, fish, lizards, rodents, rabbits, snakes, squirrels, and just about any other creature it can catch!

LIFE SPAN: 10 to 13 years in the wild; more than 30 years in captivity

STATUS: not currently threatened

The great horned owl is one of the largest owls, and its "horns" are actually tufts of feathers. A great horned owl appears much heavier than its actual weight of just a few pounds. Since its feathers help keep the great horned owl warm in winter, it does not migrate.

Because the great horned owl is such a skilled hunter, it is sometimes called a "flying tiger." Its wings, like those of other owls, have fringed flight feathers tipped with sound-deadening filaments that allow virtually silent flight, so prey never hear it swoop down from above. Great horned owls kill with their talons and sharp beak, then usually carry their meal back to their nest.

Although its beak may appear small, an owl can extend its jaws wide enough to swallow small animals whole. Twelve to 18 hours after eating, the owl regurgitates indigestible bits of prey in the form of pellets. From these pellets, scientists can determine the owl's diet.

Great horned owls have binocular vision that allows them to see distant objects. At night, their pupils open so wide that they can perceive light in what humans consider to be total darkness. Their eyes are fixed in their sockets, so they must turn their entire head in order to look around. This isn't a problem, since great horned owls have flexible necks and can turn their heads 270 degrees in either direction.

Of all birds, owls have the best hearing. Their ear holes are located beside their eyes, and the right ear hole is usually higher than the left, which allows for stereoscopic hearing. The owl's curved face acts like a parabolic dish, gathering and sending minute sounds directly to the owl's ears.

Although some farmers consider owls a nuisance because they sometimes kill chickens and turkeys, owls are a very important part of the ecosystem. In 1972 the Migratory Bird Treaty was amended to give federal protection to most birds — including owls — in North America. It is illegal to hunt, kill, or own owls.

- A young owl is called an *owlet*. A group of owls is called a *parliament*.

- Imagine you're in a dark room and can barely see anything. Now imagine that it's nine times darker. If there were a great horned owl in the room, it could see you just fine!

- Great horned owls have been known to attack humans, usually because the human is too close to the owl's nest. Owls can fly more than 40 miles per hour.

 With their binocular vision, great horned owls can easily see the small print on a newspaper a mile away. Too bad owls can't read!

 If human eyes were in proportion to those of a great horned owl, each of our eyeballs would be about the size of a grapefruit and weigh 5 pounds.

 Instead of building their own nests, great horned owls claim nests made by other animals, such as squirrels or red-tailed hawks. When young owls become old enough to keep their balance, their parents destroy the nest.

 Some owls don't give a hoot, but the great horned owl is recognized by its distinctive call, which sounds something like "Hoot-a-hoot, hoo-hoo."

 Does a great horned owl smell as well as it sees and hears? Consider this fact: It is one of the few animals that will eat a skunk.

❧ With their flexible necks, owls can easily turn their heads to look directly behind their backs.

❧ Owls are the only birds that blink by lowering their upper eyelids, just like humans. But when they go to sleep, they raise their lower eyelids to close their eyes, just like other birds.

CHEETAH

SCIENTIFIC NAME: *Acinonyx jubatus* (acinonyx means "nonretractile claws" and jubatus means "with mane")

RANGE: Africa, Middle East, and south-central Asia

HABITAT: grassy plains or savannah

YOUNG PER BIRTH: 1 to 5 cubs, but 3 is the average

BIRTH WEIGHT: 8 ounces

ADULT WEIGHT: 77 to 140 pounds

HEIGHT: 30 to 39 inches at the shoulder

BODY LENGTH: 4 to 5 feet

TAIL LENGTH: 2 to 2½ feet (half the length of its body!)

DIET: carnivorous (small antelope and gazelles)

LIFE SPAN: 10 to 12 years in the wild; up to 19 years in captivity

PREDATORS: habitat loss, hyenas, lions, and humans

STATUS: endangered. In 1900 it was estimated that there were about 100,000 cheetahs worldwide. Today estimates suggest there may be no more than 10,000 cheetahs.

🐾 In the Hindi language, *chita* means "spotted one."

🐾 Cheetah cubs remain unprotected while their mother hunts from dawn to dusk. Most cubs are eaten by lions and hyenas. It is estimated that only 1 of 20 cheetah cubs survives beyond 18 months.

🐾 The fastest of all land mammals, cheetahs can go from 0 to 45 miles per hour in 2½ seconds. They have been clocked at nearly 70 miles per hour. They can only maintain such speed for short durations, covering a distance of about 100 yards.

🐾 Because the cheetah's semiretractile claws are always "out," the cat gets a great grip on the ground when running.

🐾 Most cats sneak up and pounce on their prey. The cheetah is the only cat that runs down its prey.

🐾 The cheetah can sometimes be found perching in trees, but its long legs prevent it from being a good climber.

💥 Just as human athletes wear black paint under their eyes to minimize glare from sunlight, cheetahs have black "tear marks" under their eyes to help them see during the day.

💥 For thousands of years in Asia, cheetahs were tamed and trained for hunting, just like dogs. Unlike other big cats, cheetahs are not a threat to humans.

💥 The cheetah's long tail is slightly heavier at the end, and it helps keep the cheetah balanced during high-speed turns.

💥 The cheetah purrs but does not roar. It can also make a chirping sound that resembles a birdcall.

💥 Cheetahs share an identical DNA pattern, so all cheetahs are genetic "twins" of one another. Because of this fact, scientists believe that cheetahs were once nearly extinct, and that all currently living cheetahs are the descendents of a single pair of cheetahs.

DOMESTIC CAT

SCIENTIFIC NAME: *Felis catus* (sharp cat, as in a cunning animal)

RANGE: all over the world in rural and urban areas

HABITAT: in or around human households

YOUNG PER BIRTH: 4 is the average

BIRTH WEIGHT: 3½ to 5 ounces

ADULT WEIGHT: 6 to 15 pounds (females are smaller)

BODY LENGTH: 18 to 20 inches from the tip of the nose to the base of the tail

TAIL LENGTH: 9 inches to 15 inches (about three-quarters the length of the body)

HEIGHT: 8 to 10 inches

DIET: water, and commercial meat and dry food

LIFE SPAN: 10 to 15 years

STATUS: not threatened

❧ A male cat is called a *tom*. A female is a *queen*. A young cat is a *kitten*.

❧ There are 30 to 40 different breeds of domestic cats. The breeds are divided into two categories: the domestic shorthair and the long-haired Persian.

❧ The oldest domestic cat on record reached the age of 34 years.

❧ Using its tongue, a cat spends about 30 hours a week grooming its fur. When the cat accidentally ingests loose fur, the result is a coughed-up hair ball. Yuck!

❧ Ever seen a cat race through a house — as if it were chasing some invisible prey — at dawn or dusk? The cat is simply acting out its instinctive behavior to hunt at these hours.

❧ Got milk? Many cats are allergic to cow's milk. Some cats are allergic to fish, too.

❧ Do cats dream? Studies say they do! But cats seldom enter REM (rapid eye movement) sleep, the deep sleep in which humans and dogs dream. Instead, cats take light naps throughout the day. This allows them to wake up in an instant, completely alert!

 Some cats have extra toes. This is called *polydactylism*, an inherited trait that is passed on from a parent to a kitten.

 How does a falling cat land on its feet? When the cat falls, fluid in its inner ear shifts. The cat quickly rotates its head until the fluid is level, and the cat's body rotates with its head until its feet are aimed at the ground, ready to land!

 The tufts of a cat's ear fur are called *furnishings*.

 Kitty, come home! There have been numerous reports of lost, relocated, and abandoned cats that have traveled great distances to return to their homes. Although no one knows exactly how cats can do this, some scientists believe that cats have a natural sense of direction.

 It is estimated that there are more than 72 million pet cats in the United States. Since there are about

275 million people living in the country, that's approximately one pet cat for every four people.

☙ How many homeless cats are on the prowl in the United States? Estimates range from 40 to more than 60 million.

WHAT DO ALL CATS HAVE IN COMMON?

Cats come in all sizes, but most share the same shape and characteristics. They are all carnivores, with long canine teeth, pointed ears, and sensitive whiskers. Their jaws are hinged to open and close but don't move from side to side, so they can't grind their teeth. They generally have five toes on their front feet and four toes on their hind feet. Except for the domestic Manx and some Manx hybrids, they all have tails.

All cats have a common ancestor: *Miacis*, a weasel-like carnivore that lived about 50 million years ago and that is also the ancestor of all bears, civets, raccoons, skinks, and weasels. The cat family's scientific name is *Felidae*, and this family is divided into three groups:

1. *Felis* includes domestic house cats and all nonroaring cats except for the cheetah.
2. *Panthera* includes the cats that roar: jaguars, leopards, lions, and tigers.
3. *Acinonyx* includes only one cat, the cheetah, because it has a unique characteristic: All other cats can retract their sharp claws, but cheetah claws are blunt and do not fully retract. Thus, a cheetah's claws are always "out" and are more like the claws of a dog than a cat!

JAGUAR

SCIENTIFIC NAME: *Panthera onca* (hunter with hook, as in claws)

RANGE: southern Mexico and parts of Central and South America

HABITAT: dense forest and savannah

YOUNG PER BIRTH: 1 to 4

BIRTH WEIGHT: 25 to 32 ounces

ADULT WEIGHT: 100 to 250 pounds (females are smaller)

HEIGHT: 2½ to 3 feet

BODY LENGTH: 4 to 6 feet

TAIL LENGTH: 18 to 30 inches

DIET: carnivorous (fish, snakes, and deer)

LIFE SPAN: 11 years in the wild; up to 22 years in captivity

PREDATORS: habitat loss and humans

STATUS: vulnerable. Current estimates suggest there are just over 10,000 jaguars in the wild.

- The name jaguar comes from the South American Tupi Guarani word *yaguara*. Translations for *yaguara* vary from "he who overcomes prey in a single bound" to "the savage beast that kills with a single bite." Just remember to keep away from wild jaguars!

- The jaguar is the biggest cat native to the Americas. Of all the big cats, it is considered the best at climbing trees.

- Jaguars once existed throughout the southwestern United States. In 1860 the last jaguar in California was killed. Although there have been occasional sightings, it is believed that most wild jaguars vanished from the United States by 1950.

- During the 1960s and 1970s, an estimated 18,000 jaguars were killed for their skins.

- Although jaguars are considered "roaring" cats, their roar is more like a loud growl.

- Jaguars are one of the few species of cats that like to get wet. They are excellent swimmers.

🐾 Jaguars use their tails as lures for fish! To attract fish, the jaguar stands very still and dips its tail into the water. When a fish comes, the jaguar uses its claws to catch the fish.

🐾 Although wild jaguars live in South America and wild leopards live in Africa, people sometimes confuse jaguars and leopards. The fur of both animals is marked by *rosettes*, or roselike spots, but a jaguar has larger rosettes, and the rosettes on a jaguar's back contain smaller spots. Also, jaguars have more muscular bodies and jaws than leopards do.

🐾 Some jaguars are coated with black fur. They are called black jaguars and should not be confused with black panthers, which are actually leopards.

SCIENTIFIC NAME: *Panthera pardus* (hunter leopard)

RANGE: Africa, China, India, Siberia, and Southeast Asia

HABITAT: wooded savannah, tropical forest, and desert

YOUNG PER BIRTH: 2 cubs on average

BIRTH WEIGHT: about 1½ pounds

ADULT WEIGHT: 62 to 198 pounds (females are smaller)

HEIGHT: 17½ to 30½ inches at the shoulder

BODY LENGTH: 3½ to 5½ feet

TAIL LENGTH: 22½ to 43 inches

DIET: carnivorous (deer, gazelles, birds, and young giraffe)

LIFE SPAN: 10 to 13 years in the wild; up to 20 years in captivity

PREDATORS: lions, hyenas, and humans

STATUS: vulnerable; endangered in parts of Asia

❖ The name "leopard" comes from the Late Greek *leopardos,* which is a combination of two words: *leo* (lion) and *pard* (leopard or other large cat). In ancient times, it was believed that the leopard was part lion.

❖ A group of leopards is called a *leap.*

❖ At a glance, black panthers appear to be covered entirely in black fur, but if you look closely, their rosettes (spots) are visible. Panthers are really dark colored leopards!

❖ If a spotted leopard gives birth to a black leopard, the mother sometimes abandons the cub. Why? Because it looks different from the other cubs. Scientists have observed that black leopards that survive without any maternal guidance tend to be more fierce than other leopards.

❖ A leopard is one of the few cats that hoists its kills up into a tree. It can carry animals that weigh up to 200 pounds!

SCIENTIFIC NAME: *Panthera leo* (hunter lion)

RANGE: sub-Saharan Africa and parts of India

HABITAT: grassy plains

YOUNG PER BIRTH: 1 to 5 cubs, with an average of 3

BIRTH WEIGHT: 2 to 4½ pounds

ADULT WEIGHT: females 265 to 400 pounds; males 330 to 550 pounds

HEIGHT: female 3.6 feet; male 4 feet

BODY LENGTH: 5.6 to 6.3 feet

TAIL LENGTH: 24 to 36 inches

DIET: carnivorous (zebras, buffalo, antelope, and carrion)

LIFE SPAN: 9 to 10 years in the wild; 25 years or more in captivity

PREDATORS: humans and hyena

STATUS: vulnerable; endangered in Asia

🐾 A group of lions is called a *pride*. A pride consists of one to six adult males and two to 18 adult females and cubs. It is not unusual for a pride to contain 30 to 40 lions.

🐾 A female lion is called a *lioness*. In a pride, all the females are related.

🐾 Lions are unlike other big cats in that they are social, not solitary, creatures. They live in prides and are the only cats that hunt together. All other cats hunt alone.

🐾 In a pride, the females not only raise the cubs but also do 85 percent to 90 percent of the hunting. The males protect the pride from other male lions that want to take over.

🐾 Lions spend up to 20 hours a day sleeping. But when they're awake, look out! They can run up to 30 miles per hour and can easily bring down prey that greatly outweigh them.

🐾 With a single swipe of its powerful front paws, a lion can break a zebra's back.

🐾 Lions will steal prey captured by other animals such as cheetahs.

🐾 To get out of the sun and keep cool, lions will climb trees. They'll also climb trees to escape a stampede.

🐾 Don't invite a lion and a hyena to the same party. They really hate each other! Hyenas are one of the few creatures that will attack lions.

🐾 Lions always drink water after eating.

🐾 A lion's roar can be heard from up to 5 miles away.

MOUNTAIN LION

SCIENTIFIC NAME: *Felis concolor* (cat of the same color, or one-color cat, meaning it is without spots or stripes)

RANGE: from British Columbia through South America

HABITAT: forest, mountain, tundra, and jungle

YOUNG PER BIRTH: 1 to 6, with an average of 3 or 4

BIRTH WEIGHT: 8 to 15 ounces

ADULT WEIGHT: 80 to 200 pounds (females are smaller)

HEIGHT: 25 to 30 inches

BODY LENGTH: 3 to 4 feet

TAIL LENGTH: 24 to 36 inches

DIET: carnivorous (deer, elks, bighorn sheep, and coyotes)

LIFE SPAN: 12 years in the wild; up to 19 years in captivity

PREDATORS: humans and wolves

STATUS: endangered in some parts of the United States

- The mountain lion is known by many names, including cougar, puma, Florida panther, American ghost, Indian devil, Mexican lion, catamount (cat-of-the-mountain), deer killer, deer tiger, brown tiger, yellow tiger, red tiger, silver lion, mountain demon, mountain devil, mountain screamer, painter, purple feather, king cat, sneak cat, and panther. The term panther is incorrect, since a panther is actually a leopard. But you knew that already, right?

- Mountain lions place their hind paws into the tracks made by their front paws when they are hunting prey. Because of these careful steps, they walk with minimal noise.

- Mountain lions are one of the few creatures that will attack and eat porcupines.

- A mountain lion can kill and drag prey up to seven times its own weight.

- Incredible jumpers, mountain lions can jump — from a standing position — to a height of 18 feet and make a broad jump of 30 feet. They often attack their prey by leaping from a high rock or tree.

- The primary cause of mountain-lion death is hunting.

- The Florida panther is among the most endangered large mammals on earth. It is threatened by extreme loss of habitat.

TIGER

SCIENTIFIC NAME: *Panthera tigris* (hunter tiger)

RANGE: China, India, Russia, and Southeast Asia

HABITAT: snowy areas to tropical forests

YOUNG PER BIRTH: 2 to 4 cubs

BIRTH WEIGHT: 2 pounds

ADULT WEIGHT: 250 to more than 600 pounds (females are smaller)

HEIGHT: about 3½ feet at the shoulder

BODY LENGTH: 6 to 7 feet

TAIL LENGTH: 30 to 36 inches

DIET: carnivorous (deer, wild pigs, and buffalo)

LIFE SPAN: 15 years in the wild

PREDATORS: humans and habitat loss

STATUS: endangered. Today it is estimated there are fewer than 7,500 tigers in the world.

🐾 Tigers are the largest living cats.

🐾 The heaviest tiger is the adult male Siberian tiger, which can weigh more than 675 pounds.

🐾 Although tigers are often solitary, they sometimes hunt together and share meals.

🐾 The stripes on a tiger's face are uniquely distinctive and can be used to identify it, the same way we identify humans by their fingerprints.

🐾 If a tiger is old or has difficulty finding wild prey, it will hunt humans. These tigers are called man-eaters.

🐾 Tigers like water, and they're good swimmers, too!

🐾 Some people think tigers come from Africa, but that's just not true! Wild tigers originated in eastern Asia. As much as tigers like to swim, they can't swim the width of the entire ocean that separates China from Africa.

If you ever wondered how well you could survive on a vegetarian diet, take a look at elephants. They never eat meat, they can live long lives, and they are the largest of land mammals. They're also the second tallest, right after another herbivore: the giraffe.

There are two kinds of elephants: African elephants — including the bush elephant and the slightly smaller forest elephant — and Asian (or Indian) elephants. Each species has some differences, but they also have a lot in common. First, let's compare their statistics.

AFRICAN ELEPHANT

SCIENTIFIC NAME: *Loxodonta africana* (slanting tooth from Africa)

RANGE: central and western Africa

HABITAT: forests, swamps, grassy savannahs, and semidesert areas

YOUNG PER BIRTH: 1

BIRTH WEIGHT: 255 to 320 pounds

ADULT WEIGHT: 8,000 to 14,000 pounds

HEIGHT: up to 11 feet at the shoulder

DIET: herbivorous (all types of vegetation, including grasses, leaves, and fruit)

LIFE SPAN: 60 to 65 years

PREDATORS: humans

STATUS: threatened

ASIAN (INDIAN) ELEPHANT

SCIENTIFIC NAME: *Elephas maximus* (largest elephant, despite the fact that it's smaller than the African elephant)

RANGE: southern and southeastern Asia

HABITAT: forests and jungles

YOUNG PER BIRTH: 1

BIRTH WEIGHT: 220 pounds

ADULT WEIGHT: 7,000 to 12,000 pounds

HEIGHT: up to 9 feet at the shoulder

DIET: herbivorous (all types of vegetation, including grasses, leaves, and fruit)

LIFE SPAN: 60 to 65 years

PREDATORS: humans

STATUS: endangered

What are the differences between African and Asian elephants? The African elephant is more massive and has larger ears then the Asian elephant. The African elephant has a dip in its back, and the Asian elephant has an arched back. On closer inspection, African elephants have four or five toes on their front feet and three toes on their hind feet; Asian elephants have five toes on their front feet and four toes on their hind feet.

All elephants have a long trunk — a combination of a boneless, elongated nose and upper lip — that is composed of an estimated 40,000 muscles. The entire trunk can weigh up to 300 pounds. An African elephant's trunk ends with two fingerlike lobes, and the Asian elephant's trunk has a single fingerlike lobe. These lobes allow elephants to pick up objects as small as a single berry. With their trunks, elephants can also:

🐾 carry a 600-pound log

🐾 pluck and raise grasses and leaves to their mouths

🐾 hold and transfer 1½ gallons of water to their mouths

- spray water and give themselves a shower

- gesture and communicate with other elephants

- swim underwater, using their trunks like snorkels

- smell you more than a mile away, even if you're not especially stinky

Elephants are also distinguished by their teeth, long incisors called *tusks*, which are made of ivory. Adult African elephant males have the longest tusks; some Asian elephant males and nearly all females do not have tusks at all. Tusks are used for digging up food and for defense and also as a "rack" on which an elephant can rest its heavy trunk. Unfortunately, many people think ivory is valuable, and poachers — criminal hunters interested only in the money they can make from an elephant's tusks — have killed countless elephants.

In the early twentieth century it was estimated that the elephant population consisted of more than 5 million elephants. Today estimates range from 300,000 to 600,000 African elephants in the wild and possibly fewer than 50,000 Asian elephants. Since 1989 the U.S. government has officially banned African elephant ivory from being imported into the country. African elephants are still threatened by poachers, and both African and Asian elephants are endangered by habitat loss.

❈ The word *elephant* comes from the Greek word for ivory, *elephas*.

❈ An adult female elephant is called a *cow*, and an adult male elephant is called a *bull*. A group of elephants is called a *herd* or *host*.

❈ A baby elephant is called a *calf*. A calf can walk within one hour after birth.

❈ Elephant families are made up of elephant mothers and their offspring, and they are led by the eldest female, called the *matriarch*. When male elephants become adults, they leave the family but sometimes return for a visit.

❈ Elephants have poor vision and have difficulty seeing distant, nonmoving objects. However, they compensate with exceptional hearing and smell.

Elephants can make low-frequency sound waves that can't be heard by human ears but can be detected by other elephants miles away. Elephants use these sounds to stay in contact with their own herd and other herds.

In the wild, elephants spend about 16 hours a day eating. An adult elephant eats about 300 to 500 pounds of vegetation daily and drinks up to 40 gallons of water.

Elephants grow throughout their lifetime, and males grow more than females. A 40-year-old male elephant can be nearly twice the size of a 40-year-old female elephant.

An African bull claims the record for longest tusk: 11 feet 6 inches.

Elephants are often called *pachyderms*, meaning thick-skinned. Indeed, the skin at an elephant's shoulder can be about 1½ inches thick, but it is quite tender. Elephants take frequent baths and coat themselves with dust to prevent mosquitoes from biting them.

❧ Elephants do not have sweat glands, and they flap their ears to keep cool.

❧ Besides the elephant, the only other animal that has ivory tusks is the walrus, which is also a threatened species.

❧ The first elephant brought to America was a two-year-old female that arrived in New York on April 13, 1796. She had been purchased in India for $450 by Captain Jacob Crowninshield of Salem, Massachusetts. Crowninshield sold her for $10,000 to a businessman who wanted to display the elephant in a traveling exhibit. Known only as "The Elephant," she toured the northeastern states continuously for at least 16 years.

❧ An elephant's brain weighs about 11 pounds and is four times the size of a human brain. But if a human's head were as big as an elephant's head, the elephant's brain would be one-tenth the size of the human brain.

❧ An adult elephant's heart weighs more than 25 pounds. At approximately 28 beats per minute, an elephant's heartbeat is the slowest of all mammals.

☙ The largest African elephant on record was a bull that weighed more than 13½ tons and was shot on November 7, 1974, in Angola. Lying on the ground, his height was estimated to have been 13 feet.

JUMBO

Jumbo the Elephant had been the star attraction at the London Zoo for more than two decades when the legendary showman P. T. Barnum bought him for $10,000 in 1882. At the time, Jumbo was 10 feet 10 inches tall, weighed 8 tons, and was called "the Largest Elephant on Earth." Barnum brought Jumbo to America, and their tour eventually brought them to Ontario, Canada. There, on September 15, 1885, Jumbo was on a train track when he was struck and killed by a freight train.

Barnum hired the world-renowned taxidermists Professor Henry Augustus Ward and Carl Akeley to mount Jumbo's skin onto a custom-made elephant-shaped wooden frame. It took almost two years to make the Jumbo "dummy." After exhibiting Jumbo's mounted hide for four years, Barnum donated it to Tufts University. He also donated Jumbo's skeleton to the American Museum of Natural History.

Jumbo's name originated from the Swahili word *jumbe*, meaning chief. Today the word *jumbo* lives on as anything that's very big.

SCIENTIFIC NAME: *Macropus canguru* (bigfoot kangaroo)

RANGE: Tasmania and eastern and southwestern Australia

HABITAT: open forests

YOUNG PER BIRTH: 1

BIRTH WEIGHT: .03 ounce — about the size of a jelly bean!

ADULT WEIGHT: average 150 pounds, but up to 200 pounds (females are smaller)

HEIGHT: up to 6 feet

LENGTH: up to 10 feet from nose to tip of tail

TAIL LENGTH: 4 to 4½ feet

DIET: herbivorous (grass and leaves)

LIFE SPAN: 5 years in the wild; 18 years in captivity

PREDATORS: humans

STATUS: gray kangaroos are not threatened, but other kangaroo species are vulnerable, and several species are extinct

There's a popular story about how the kangaroo got its name. Legend says that when European explorers asked an Australian Aborigine to identify the strange, hopping animals, the Aborigine answered, *"Kangaroo."* The Europeans accepted this as the species' name and did not realize that the Aboriginal word *kangaroo* meant "I do not understand you."

That story might be amusing, and it has even appeared in several history books, but . . . *it's not true*!

In 1770 the English explorer Captain Cook arrived at the continent we now call Australia with the naturalist Sir Joseph Banks, the first European to record the word *kangooroo* (Banks's original spelling). An Aboriginal word, it came from the Guugu Yimidhirr language and was the specific name for the black kangaroo. Cook and his party mistakenly believed that *kangooroo* applied to all similarly hopping creatures.

In the mammal family *Macropodidae* (big feet), there are 47 species of kangaroos, and the gray kangaroo — also known as *forester* — is one of the largest. Kangaroos also happen to be the largest *marsupials*. For more about marsupials, read on!

- A baby kangaroo is called a *joey*. A joey is born in a still-embryonic state and spends seven to eight months growing inside its mother's pouch.

- Female kangaroos are called *fliers*. Male kangaroos are called *boomers*.

- Kangaroos live in social groups called *mobs*. Generally, the females outnumber the males five to one.

- There's some disagreement over whether the gray kangaroo is bigger than the red kangaroo. The red kangaroo is sometimes taller, but the gray kangaroo tends to be heavier.

- The gray kangaroo can easily maintain a cruising speed of 25 miles per hour and go up to 40 miles per hour for short distances. It can jump a distance of 25 feet and a height of 10 feet.

- A kangaroo uses its tail as a support when it stands and for balance when it hops.

- Because of their large tails, kangaroos cannot move backward very easily.

☙ Kangaroos require little water and can go for months without drinking.

☙ Even when hopping, kangaroos hardly break a sweat. They keep their cool by breathing very fast, up to 300 breaths per minute.

WHAT'S A MARSUPIAL?

The word marsupial comes from *marsupium*, the Latin word for pouch. Indeed, most female marsupials have an external abdominal pouch they use to shelter their babies, but some marsupials — such as the wombat and the short-tailed opossum — do not have pouches.

So what do marsupials have in common? Unlike other mammals, a marsupial mother gives birth early, when the baby is quite small and undeveloped. Amazingly, the tiny baby manages to attach to its mother's nipple and get nourishment. With kangaroos, the joey grows inside the mother's pouch. Several months later, the joey is fully developed and can leave the pouch.

SCIENTIFIC NAME: *Sus scrofa* (in Latin, *sus* means pig and *scrofa* is breeding sow)

RANGE: every continent but Antarctica

HABITAT: family and factory farms

YOUNG PER BIRTH: up to 12, but 5 or 6 is average

BIRTH WEIGHT: about 2½ pounds

ADULT WEIGHT: 300 to 700 pounds, and more!

DIET: corn, oats, soybeans, and edible garbage

LIFE SPAN: 15 years or more, but most are slaughtered at 6 months

PREDATORS: humans

STATUS: not threatened by extinction, but some breeds are at risk

In the United States, the eight most common breeds of pigs are the American Landrace, Berkshire, Chester White, Duroc, Hampshire, Poland China, Spotted Swine, and Yorkshire. Of these breeds, the Hampshire is the most abundant.

🐾 A male pig is a *boar*. A young female pig is a *gilt*. An adult female pig is a *sow*. A baby pig is a *piglet*. A group of pigs is a *drove, herd*, or *sounder*.

🐾 Within six months, a piglet can grow to 220 pounds.

🐾 When a domestic pig reaches a weight of about 180 pounds, it is considered ready for market and is called a *hog*.

🐾 Hogs eat about 20 percent of all the corn grown in the United States annually.

🐾 Do you sweat like a pig? If you do, then you must not sweat at all, because pigs don't have working sweat glands!

🐾 Since pigs can't perspire, they keep cool by wallowing (rolling about) in mud. The mud also protects against sunburn and bug bites.

❧ Despite the fact that pigs cover themselves in mud, they prefer to keep themselves clean. Given a choice between mud or wading in freshwater, they'll go for the water. What's more, they're very good swimmers!

❧ People with life-threatening diseases sometimes benefit from organ transplants. Because human "parts" are not always available for transplantation, scientists have looked to nonhuman alternatives such as pigs. Since the 1960s, pig aortic heart valves have been transplanted into humans who have severe heart disease. Transplanting organs from one species to another is called *xenotransplantation*.

❧ Pigs have a great sense of smell and have been trained to sniff out truffles, an edible fungus that grows underground, usually near oak trees. However, dogs are more often used as truffle hunters. Why? Because truffles can be worth more than $500 per pound, and pigs — unlike dogs — won't hesitate to eat the truffles they unearth.

EASTERN COTTONTAIL RABBIT

SCIENTIFIC NAME: *Sylvilagus floridanus* ("woods hare" of Florida)

RANGE: North and Central America

HABITAT: meadows and farmlands

YOUNG PER BIRTH: 2 to 8, with an average of 5

BIRTH WEIGHT: about 1 ounce

ADULT WEIGHT: 2 to 4 pounds

LENGTH: 12 to 20 inches

EAR LENGTH: 2½ to 3 inches

TAIL LENGTH: 1 to 2 inches

DIET: herbivorous (wild grasses, twigs and woody plants, and vegetables)

LIFE SPAN: 15 months to 2 years in the wild; up to 10 years in captivity

PREDATORS: foxes, owls, hawks, large snakes, and humans

STATUS: not threatened

There are eight species of cottontail rabbits in North America, the most common of which is the eastern cottontail. The others are the New England cottontail, desert cottontail, mountain cottontail, pygmy rabbit, marsh rabbit, swamp rabbit, and brush rabbit. All are considered game animals.

 A female rabbit is a *doe*. A male rabbit is a *buck*. A group of rabbits is called a *herd*.

 Eastern cottontails are born in litters of two to eight. An eastern cottontail doe usually has two to four litters each year. Cottontails in warmer climates can have up to six or seven litters each year.

 Baby cottontails do not remain babies for very long. They usually reach maturity within six months.

 If over the course of one year a cottontail buck and doe have four litters and each litter has five babies, that's 20 babies in one year, right? If the parents' offspring follow their lead, and their offsprings' offspring do the same, the result would be 168,420 cottontails (not including the original parents) within five years. That's a lot of bunnies!

- Many animals prey on cottontails. It is estimated that 75 percent of wild cottontails die before their fifth month, and they rarely live past two years.

- In the United States, rabbits are second only to deer as the most hunted animals.

- To escape a predator, a cottontail will make a series of quick zigzag moves. This rapid movement is called *flushing*. When flushing, a cottontail can reach a speed of up to 18 miles per hour.

- Cottontails will also evade predators by jumping into a lake or stream. Fortunately, cottontails are good swimmers!

RABBITS OR HARES?

Both rabbits and hares are *lagomorphs*, gnawing animals that are similar in appearance. Generally, hares have larger bodies and longer ears, which are often black-tipped.

Hares are usually solitary, but rabbits (excluding cottontails) sometimes gather in groups. Hares are also better adapted for running. Some hares can reach speeds of about 50 miles per hour!

SCIENTIFIC NAME: *Phoca vitulina* ("sea wolf," or "sea dog")

RANGE: North Atlantic and North Pacific oceans

HABITAT: ocean shores

YOUNG PER BIRTH: 1

BIRTH WEIGHT: 18 to 26 pounds

ADULT WEIGHT: 100 to 250 pounds (females are smaller)

LENGTH: 4 to 6 feet

DIET: carnivorous (fish, shrimps, squid, and octopuses)

LIFE SPAN: 20 to 25 years

PREDATORS: killer whales and polar bears

STATUS: not endangered, but protected in U.S. waters by the Marine Mammal Protection Act

The harbor seal is a *pinniped*, an aquatic, fin-footed mammalian carnivore. The word *pinniped* is a combination of the Latin words *pinna* (wing) and *ped* (foot). There are three members of the pinniped family: walruses, seals with earflaps, and seals without earflaps. Harbor seals don't have earflaps, but they do have ears! Their ears are simply small openings in the skin.

- A male seal is a *bull*. A female seal is a *cow*. A baby seal is a *pup*.

- A group of seals is called a *pod*. Although seals gather in pods, they are mostly solitary animals.

- Harbor seal pups are usually born on a reef or sandbar. They can swim almost immediately after birth.

- Harbor seals propel themselves with their hind limbs and steer with their front limbs, which is the opposite of the method employed by sea lions. Seals can easily swim at a speed of 6 miles per hour but can reach a speed of 18 miles per hour for short durations.

🐾 Harbor seals can dive to depths of 300 feet and stay underwater for up to 28 minutes. An average hunting dive takes them only 50 feet deep and lasts just several minutes.

🐾 Although harbor seals are graceful and swift in the water, they do not move around easily on land. Because they are unable to turn their hind flippers forward, they cannot raise their bodies on land, so they move by squirming like a caterpillar!

🐾 An adult harbor seal consumes 10 to 18 pounds of food a day. That's about 5 to 6 percent of its total body weight.

🐾 Harbor seals can sleep underwater or float in an upright position called *bottling*, with their heads poking up above the water's surface.

CALIFORNIA SEA LION

SCIENTIFIC NAME: *Zalophus californianus* (zalophus is a combination of two Greek words: *Za*, an intensive prefix, and *lophus*, which means "crest" and refers to the high bony crest on the adult male sea lion's skull)

RANGE: coasts of southern California and northwestern Mexico

HABITAT: ocean shores

YOUNG PER BIRTH: 1

BIRTH WEIGHT: 13 pounds

ADULT WEIGHT: 110 to 850 pounds (females are smaller)

LENGTH: 6 to 8 feet

DIET: carnivorous (fish, mollusks, and crustaceans)

LIFE SPAN: up to 30 years

PREDATORS: killer whales, great white sharks, and humans

STATUS: not endangered, but protected in U.S. waters by the Marine Mammal Protection Act

- A male sea lion is a *bull*. A female sea lion is a *cow*. A baby sea lion is a *pup*.

- During mating season, sea lions form a *harem*. The harem contains one bull and up to 20 cows.

- Like harbor seals, sea lion pups are born on land, but unlike seals they do not immediately take to the water. Sea lion pups are usually about two months old when they start swimming.

- Sea lions propel themselves with their powerful front flippers and steer with their hind flippers. They are the fastest pinnipeds, with bursts of speed up to 30 miles per hour, but they usually cruise at about 11 miles per hour. They also like to bodysurf!

- California sea lions can dive to depths of 1,000 feet and remain submerged for 10 to 15 minutes.

- Unlike harbor seals, California sea lions can turn their hind flippers forward, which allows them to walk on land.

🐾 California sea lions are very social and enjoy being in groups.

🐾 Performing seals at zoos and aquariums are usually California sea lions. They are very intelligent.

LITTLE BROWN BAT

SCIENTIFIC NAME: *Myotis lucifugus* (*myotis* means mouse-eared, and *lucifugus* means light-fleeing)

RANGE: throughout North America

HABITAT: caves, tree hollows, and buildings

YOUNG PER BIRTH: 1

BIRTH WEIGHT: about .075 to .105 ounces

ADULT WEIGHT: .25 to .35 ounces (females are slightly larger)

HEIGHT: 3.1 to 3.7 inches from nose to tip of tail

WINGSPAN: 8.6 to 10.6 inches

DIET: insectivorous (mosquitoes, beetles, gnats, wasps, and moths)

LIFE SPAN: average 5 years in the wild, but some more than 30 years!

PREDATORS: hawks, owls, and raccoons

STATUS: no special status

There are more than 900 species of bats, and they account for nearly one-fourth of *all* mammals! Most bats are nocturnal, making their homes in caves or tree cavities and sleeping upside down with their feet clinging to a rock or branch. Many bats eat insects or fruit, but some are carnivorous.

The little brown bat is the most common bat in North America. Although the little brown bat is not endangered, it is estimated that 40 percent of North American bats are threatened or endangered.

🐾 Bats are the only mammals that can truly fly. The little brown bat can maintain a flight speed of about 12 miles per hour.

🐾 A young bat is called a *pup*. At birth, a pup may weigh 25 to 30 percent of the mother's weight, which is pretty amazing. That's like a 130-pound human female giving birth to a 39-pound baby. Yikes!

🐾 Little brown bats can fly when they're three weeks old. They reach their adult weight at four weeks.

🐾 Like whales and dolphins, most bats use *echolocation* — a form of built-in sonar — to navigate and find prey in the dark. A bat emits sound pulses that bounce off objects and produce echoes, which return to the bat's ears. From these echoes, the bat can "visualize" its surroundings as well as the size and location of prey.

* Little brown bats hunt for about two hours after sunset and two hours before sunrise. Within an hour, a little brown bat can catch 600 mosquitoes.

* Have you ever heard the expression "blind as a bat"? Well, bats are *not* visually impaired and actually see very well!

RABIES

All mammals can carry *rabies,* a deadly viral disease. Animals that are not mammals (birds, lizards, and fish) do not carry rabies. Mammals with rabies are called *rabid,* and rabies is carried in their saliva, not their blood. Mammals usually get rabies by being bitten by rabid mammals.

Rabid wild mammals usually behave differently from healthy wild mammals. Rabid mammals may move very slowly and act as if they are tame. If you see a raccoon, skunk, bat, fox, cat, dog, or any other mammal behaving oddly, do not touch it or go near it!

If you are bitten by any animal that might have rabies, you should clean the wound with soap and water right away and then see a doctor immediately. There is a vaccine that will prevent death from rabies.

DOMESTIC DOG

SCIENTIFIC NAME: *Canis familiaris* (familiar dog)

RANGE: worldwide

HABITAT: in or around human households

YOUNG PER BIRTH: 1 to 4 for small breeds; 4 to 8 for medium breeds; 6 to 10 for large breeds

BIRTH WEIGHT: 3½ ounces to 1 pound

ADULT WEIGHT: tiny dogs: 1 to 9 pounds
    small dogs: 10 to 19 pounds
    medium-size dogs: 20 to 49 pounds
    large dogs: 50 to 90 pounds
    huge dogs: 91 to 175 pounds and more!

HEIGHT: 5 inches to 39 inches at the shoulder

DIET: dry and canned dog food, water

LIFE SPAN: 10 to 15 years (smaller dogs live longer)

PREDATORS: other dogs

STATUS: no special status

Like cats, dogs can trace their ancestry to an animal called *Miacis*, which lived about 50 million years ago. A more direct ancestor is *Tomarctus*, which resembled a wolf and lived about 15 million years ago. Coyotes, foxes, jackals, and wolves are also the descendents of Tomarctus. All members of the dog family are *digitigrade*, meaning they walk on their toes. Scientists believe that dogs were domesticated as far back as 10,000 years ago, which makes them the oldest known domestic animal.

Domestic dogs can be either *purebred* or *mixed breed*. A purebred is a dog whose parents and ancestors were of the same breed, so purebreds greatly resemble their parents. A mixed-breed — also called a *mongrel* or *mutt* — is a dog whose parents were not of the same breed, so every mixed-breed dog has unique characteristics.

There are about 400 breeds of purebreds, of which the American Kennel Club recognizes seven different groups:

Sporting dogs hunt, point out, or retrieve game birds.

Hounds hunt all game except for birds.

Working dogs guard property, pull sleds, and do rescue work.

Terriers are now house pets but were originally bred to drive off rodents.

Toy dogs are tiny dogs.

Nonsporting dogs are purebreds that are not included in the other categories.

Herding dogs protect farm animals from predators and prevent them from straying.

🐾 A young dog that nurses off its mother's milk is a *whelp*, which is also a term that means "to give birth to dogs." Whelps born at the same time to the same mother are called a *litter*. A young dog is also a *pup* or *puppy*.

🐾 Most whelps are up and walking within two to three weeks. When a whelp is about six weeks old, it is *weaned*, meaning it stops nursing from its mother.

🐾 Dogs' body cells contain 39 pairs of chromosomes, the most of any mammal! Chromosomes are heredity-carrying structures that ensure consistent traits so that offspring will resemble their parents. Human body cells contain 23 pairs of chromosomes.

On November 3, 1957, the Soviet Union launched the satellite *Sputnik II*, a space capsule that carried an 11-pound female dog. Although her Russian trainers called her Kudryavka (Little Curly), she became known by the name of her breed: Laika (Barker). She was reported to have been a stray and selected because it was believed that a stray would be more immune than a pet to cold and hunger.

Inside the capsule's pressurized chamber, Laika had a food supply and wore a rubber bag around her hindquarters to collect waste. She became the first animal to orbit Earth.

Unfortunately for Laika, it was a one-way trip. Since Russian rocket scientists had not yet figured out how to bring *Sputnik II* safely back to Earth, the official "plan" was that Laika would die when her air supply ran out. Although Russian officials maintained that Laika lived for an entire week in space, other reports suggest that a malfunction in the capsule's heating system caused her to die from heat exhaustion within two days. *Sputnik II*'s orbit ended on April 14, 1958, when it reentered and burned up in Earth's atmosphere.

🐾 The smallest dog is the chihuahua, which stands about 5 inches high at the shoulder and weighs about 5 pounds.

🐾 The heaviest dogs are Saint Bernards and mastiffs, which can weigh 200 pounds.

* The tallest dogs are Great Danes and Irish wolfhounds, which can stand 39 inches at the shoulder.

* Greyhounds are bred to run fast and are considered the fastest dog, reaching speeds of 45 miles per hour.

* Unlike cats, dogs cannot retract their claws.

* Why do dogs pant? It helps them keep cool! Dogs have sweat glands on their feet, but these glands don't affect a dog's body temperature much.

* Why do dogs dig? A domestic dog's wild ancestors used to dig holes to hide its food from other animals. Over many centuries, dogs have kept this instinctive behavior.

GRAY WOLF

SCIENTIFIC NAME: *Canis lupis* (dog wolf)

HABITAT: extremely variable: forests, mountains, and arctic tundra

RANGE: North America, Europe, Asia, and Middle East

YOUNG PER BIRTH: 4 to 6

BIRTH WEIGHT: 1 pound

ADULT WEIGHT: up to 175 pounds, but 75 to 125 pounds is average (females are smaller)

HEIGHT: 27 to 31 inches at the shoulder

BODY LENGTH: 3 to 5 feet

TAIL LENGTH: 1 to 2 feet

DIET: carnivorous (elks, deer, bison, moose, and caribou)

LIFE SPAN: 10 to 12 years in the wild; up to 18 years in captivity

PREDATORS: golden eagles and bears prey on very young wolves; an adult wolf's only predators are humans

STATUS: endangered and threatened

The gray wolf is also known as the timber wolf, arctic wolf, and tundra wolf. Before European colonization, gray wolves roamed most of North America. In the nineteenth century the U.S. government sponsored the killing of wolves as "predator control."

In 1967 gray wolves were recognized as an endangered species in the United States, but they are still hunted and trapped in other countries. Scientists have identified 23 subspecies of the gray wolf, but only about 15 subspecies still exist. Their population remains endangered.

- A group of wolves is called a *pack* or *rout*. There are usually seven to eight members in a pack. The pack leaders are the two most dominant members, the alpha male and the alpha female.

- The entire pack — males and females — cares for young pups.

- How do wolves sleep in subzero temperatures? They tuck their faces under their legs and use their thick tails like a blanket to cover themselves.

- A wolf can smell its prey up to three-quarters of a mile away.

- Wolves can easily maintain a trotting speed of about 5 miles per hour for several hours and can travel up to 30 miles in a single night. When chasing prey, they can reach speeds of up to 45 miles per hour.

- Wolves have very strong jaws that can crush the bones of their prey.

- Although all members of the pack — except for young pups — participate in the hunt, a single wolf can be strong enough to kill a large moose.

- Despite what you may have heard in stories, wolves do not howl at the moon. They howl to locate or round up other pack members and to declare their territory to other wolf packs.

- Are you afraid of the big, bad wolf? You should know that there's no such thing as the big, bad wolf, and wolves are afraid of humans! There is no record of a person ever being attacked by a healthy, unprovoked wolf in North America.

SCIENTIFIC NAME: *Vulpes vulpes* (fox fox)

RANGE: throughout North America, Europe, and Asia; introduced to Australia in the nineteenth century

HABITAT: forest, prairie, farmland, and suburbs

YOUNG PER BIRTH: 1 to 13, with an average of 5

BIRTH WEIGHT: 4 ounces

ADULT WEIGHT: 8 to 15 pounds (females are smaller)

HEIGHT: 14 to 16 inches at the shoulder

BODY LENGTH: 22 to 32 inches from nose to rump

TAIL LENGTH: 14 to 16 inches (about half its body length!)

DIET: omnivorous (mice, rabbits, insects, fruits, and carrion)

LIFE SPAN: up to 14 years, but 5 years is average

PREDATORS: humans and coyotes

STATUS: no special status

✤ There are four species of foxes in North America: the red, gray, arctic, and swift fox. The red fox is the most common species and covers the greatest range.

✤ A male fox is called a *dog* or *reynard*. A female fox is a *vixen*. A newborn fox is a *kit, cub*, or *pup*. A group of foxes is called a *skulk* or *band*.

✤ Both parents care for their young. The red fox father provides food for his mate and their pups.

✤ Red foxes can reach speeds of about 30 miles per hour and can leap over obstacles as high as 6½ feet.

✤ Foxes are often raised or trapped for their pelts, which are used to make fur coats.

✤ Although foxes are related to dogs, they share some characteristics with cats: The pupils of their eyes are vertical slits, their claws are partially retractable, and their bodies are relatively light. Also, when foxes hunt, they stalk and pounce on their prey, much like a cat does.

- The fox's tail is called a *brush*. Like the wolf, a fox will cover its head with its tail to keep warm.

- Unlike wolves, red foxes are solitary and do not form packs.

- What do foxes have in common with ravens? Like ravens, they will follow wolves in the hope of getting leftovers from their prey. However, wolves will attack foxes, so foxes usually keep their distance.

- Although red foxes will share their territory with wolves, they move on if threatened by coyotes. Why? Coyotes don't like foxes and will kill them even if they're not especially hungry.

SCIENTIFIC NAME: *Canis latrans* (barking dog)

RANGE: all over North America (except for the northernmost regions of Canada), Mexico, and Central America

HABITAT: open grassland and wooded areas

YOUNG PER BIRTH: 2 to 12, with an average of 6

BIRTH WEIGHT: ½ pound

ADULT WEIGHT: 15 to 45 pounds

HEIGHT: 12 to 22 inches at the shoulder

BODY LENGTH: 30 to 40 inches

TAIL LENGTH: 12 to 16 inches

DIET: carnivorous (birds, snakes, carrion, but also fruits and vegetables)

LIFE SPAN: up to 15 years in the wild; 22 years in captivity

PREDATORS: humans

STATUS: the species is not threatened, but it is protected in 12 states

- The name *"coyote"* is Mexican Spanish, derived from the Nahuatl word *coyotl.*

- Male and female coyotes share the responsibility of raising their young. The father brings food to the mother and young pups, and the mother moves her pups from one den to another if she senses danger.

- Before 1900, coyotes were found only west of the Mississippi River. Today the coyote has the widest distribution of any wild mammal in North America. Scientists believe this is the direct result of wolves — who kill coyotes — having been eliminated in so many areas.

- In 1995 a pair of coyotes was found in New York City! Maybe they took the subway. . . .

- The coyote is considered the most vocal nonhuman mammal and has three distinct calls: a high-pitched squeak, distress call, and howl call.

- Estimates suggest that 5 percent to 20 percent of coyote pups don't survive their first year in the wild.

🐾 Although they are essentially carnivores, coyotes will eat whatever is available. If they can't find meat, they'll eat fruit, so they are sometimes considered omnivorous.

🐾 In urban areas, coyotes will eat pet cats and small dogs. If there are coyotes in your area, make sure your pets are protected!

🐾 Coyotes are capable of breeding with wolves and domestic dogs. The offspring of a dog and a coyote is called a *coydog*.

SPOTTED HYENA

SCIENTIFIC NAME: *Crocuta crocuta* (*crocus* is the color of saffron and *utus* means "provided with")

RANGE: sub-Saharan Africa

HABITAT: open country and semidesert

YOUNG PER BIRTH: 2

BIRTH WEIGHT: 3 pounds

ADULT WEIGHT: 120 to 189 pounds (females are larger)

LENGTH: 37 to 65 inches including tail

TAIL LENGTH: 12 inches

HEIGHT: 27 to 36 inches

DIET: carnivorous (wildebeests, gazelles, and zebras)

LIFE SPAN: 12 years in the wild; up to 41 years in captivity

PREDATORS: lions and humans

STATUS: not listed

Spotted hyenas are members of the family *Hyaenidae*, which also includes the striped hyena, the brown hyena (which is endangered), and the aardwolf. Although hyenas resemble dogs, scientists believe that they are more closely related to the cat and the mongoose.

Like dogs, hyenas have blunt claws that are incapable of being retracted, but unlike dogs, they only have four toes on each paw.

- A group of hyenas is called a *clan*. A hyena clan can have up to 70 members.

- Female hyenas are the dominant leaders of a clan. If a female and male hyena fight over food, the female usually wins.

- For many years, people believed that hyenas were primarily scavengers that fed off the leftovers of other animals. In fact, they are very skilled hunters that kill most of their own meals.

- When pursuing prey, the hyena can maintain a speed of 32 miles per hour for several miles and has been clocked at speeds of up to 37 miles per hour.

- In proportion to its size, the hyena may have the most powerful jaws of any mammal. It can eat large bones, horns, and even the teeth of its prey.

- Hyena cubs nurse from their mother for up to 16 months and do not eat food during this time. The mother's milk is rich in calcium because she eats bones.

- An individual hyena can eat about 32 pounds of prey at one sitting. After consuming so much, the hyena will take a break from killing and eating for several days.

- Although hyenas eat their prey's entire body, they can't digest every bit, so they disgorge indigestible hair, horns, hooves, and bones. Hyenas are the only mammals that routinely disgorge food this way. In fact, their digestive habits are most similar to owls'!

- Do you think hyenas are funny? The spotted hyena is also known as the "laughing hyena" because it produces what sounds like a maniacal laugh when it is distressed.

SCIENTIFIC NAME: *Equus caballus* (packhorse)

RANGE: Africa, Asia, Australia, Europe, and North and South America (range includes both wild and domesticated)

HABITAT: most horses are domestic, but there are still feral horses that exist in diverse habitats

YOUNG PER BIRTH: 1 (2 is rare)

BIRTH WEIGHT: varies by breed, but averages between 50 and 65 pounds

ADULT WEIGHT: ponies: under 900 pounds
    light horses: 900 to 1,100 pounds
    heavy horses: more than 1,100 pounds

HEIGHT: 2 feet to more than 6 feet, measured at the withers, the highest point on its back

DIET: herbivorous (wild: grass; domesticated: hay, grass, and grain)

LIFE SPAN: 20 to 40 years

PREDATORS: wild horses are prey to wolves, wild dogs, large cats, and other animals

STATUS: domestic horses are not endangered, but wild horses are

During the Ice Age, horses lived throughout North America, Europe, Asia, and Africa, where they were hunted by humans for meat. After the Ice Age (about 7,000 years ago), horses almost became extinct, with only a small population left in central Asia.

Scientists believe horses were first domesticated about 6,000 years ago. It is almost impossible to imagine history without horses. They have been used for work, pleasure, transportation, and even war.

On March 13, 1519, Spanish explorer Hernán Cortés arrived near Vera Cruz, Mexico. Cortés had brought 16 horses, and these were the first horses to walk on the North American continent in several thousand years. More explorers and more horses followed. In 1540, during an expedition led by explorer Francisco Vásquez de Coronado, a large number of horses escaped in Arizona. It is believed that these escaped domestic horses were the first "wild" horses in North America.

🐾 A newborn horse — male or female — is a *foal*. A young male horse is also called a *colt*, and a young female horse is a *filly*. A young horse between the ages of one and two years is a *year-*

ling. An adult male horse is a *stallion*, and an adult female horse is a *mare.*

🐾 Contained within a building used to shelter and feed animals, a group of horses is called a *stable* (this word also refers to the shelter itself). A group of workhorses is called a *team*. A group of racehorses that belongs to a single owner is a *string*. Racehorses that compete against one another in a group is a *field.*

🐾 There are more than 150 different breeds of horses. Przewalski's horse — named after its discoverer, the Russian explorer General Nikolai Michailovitch Przewalski — is the only surviving species of wild horse.

🐾 A horse that has never been broken (saddled or harnessed) is called a *bronco.*

🐾 A horse's left side is called the *near side.* A horse's right side is called the *off side* or *far side.* According to riding etiquette, the rider always mounts (climbs on) and dismounts (climbs off) the horse on the near side.

- A horse's size is measured at the *withers* — an elevated part of the spine between the neck and the back. The measurement is made in *hands*, a system derived from the average width of a human hand. One hand equals 4 inches.

- There are five basic body colors for horses: bay (a mixture of red and yellow), black, brown, chestnut (reddish), and white. Color variations include dun (yellowish), gray, palomino (golden), and pinto (irregular white).

- There are three types of horses: ponies, light horses, and heavy horses. Ponies are under 14 hands (56 inches). Light horses are 14 to 16 hands (56 to 64 inches). Heavy horses are more than 16 hands (64 inches).

- Ponies do not "grow" into horses. Ponies *are* horses! It's just their relatively smaller size that makes them ponies.

- The smallest horse breed is the Falabella, which has an average height of 30 to 32½ inches (about 8 hands) at the withers, with some as small as 23 inches.

- One of the largest horse breeds is the Shire, which stands up to 76 inches (19 hands) at the withers and weighs around 2,000 pounds. A single Shire is capable of hauling a 5-ton load.

- Quarter horses got their name because they can run a quarter mile faster than any other breed, reaching speeds of 38 to 40 miles per hour. Because they can start, stop, and turn very quickly, they are used as racehorses and in polo matches.

- The horse breed known as Thoroughbred originated when three Arabian stallions — the Darley Arabian, the Godolphin Barb, and the Byerly Turk — were bred with English mares in England at the turn of the seventeenth century. All American Thoroughbreds can trace their ancestry to those three stallions!

- Healthy Thoroughbreds can maintain a speed of 30 miles per hour for several miles.

- A horse's teeth are permanent, and the degree of wear (from eating) can determine a horse's age. A mature male horse has 40 teeth. A mature female has 36 teeth. A male or female foal has 24 teeth.

🐾 Ever heard the expression "Don't look a gift horse in the mouth"? The expression means that you should be grateful for a gift and not question whether you're receiving something that's too old to still be useful.

What You Don't Know About the Author

Ryder Windham was born in Watertown, New York, on June 19, 1964, the same day that the U.S. Senate passed the Civil Rights bill, and the Beatles released their recording of "Long Tall Sally." Since third grade, he has been able to recite the alphabet backward faster than he can say it forward. Whenever he eats pumpernickel bread or raw carrots, he hiccoughs. He has written numerous Star Wars children's books and comic book scripts, and collaborated with artist Killian Plunkett on the comic series Trouble Magnet: The Adventures of Witlock the Robot. He doesn't think there's anything wrong with keeping a dictionary next to your bed in case you need to look up words in the middle of the night. He lives with his family in Providence, Rhode Island.